Mockups 101

A Better Way to Discuss
Software Requirements

Igor Ješe

"Best practices, easy to follow and to apply."

"A short book that distills the essence of why and when mockups should be used."

"Lessons learned in the real world to help you use mockups in your career."

"Simple, easy to follow suggestions that just make good sense."

"Great simple straight forward approach to using mockups."

"The concepts are well thought-out and the examples are equally wonderful."

The most up-to-date version of this book can be read for FREE online, accessible from this web-page: http://www.mockups101.com

Table of Contents

PART I: CREATING AND USING MOCKUPS

About This Book

This book is about using mockups as a way to agree on the functionality of a software system or website. Mockups visually represent the system before it's been built, but what makes the biggest difference is how you actually *use* those mockups.

This is not a "How-to" book. Rather, it is composed of stories and topics based on my own experiences and revelations that I've had over more than a decade of extensively using mockups and wireframes for numerous IT projects, both big and small.

I've worked hard to keep this book short, for a simple reason: if it's short, it's more likely to actually be used.

Who Should Read This Book

I've written this book primarily with IT analysts and consultants in mind. However, other people should also find this book useful, including web programmers, designers, and solo developers, to mention a few.

This book should help you if you want to:

- Get early feedback from clients.

- Use mockups to improve communication between customers and developers.

- Avoid (or solve) common problems encountered in a wide variety of different situations.

How This Book is Structured

I have separated this book in two parts, each having a different purpose.

Chapters in Part I describe the way I create and use mockups. I don't claim to have all the answers (because I don't), but the process explained here has worked for me very well over the years. You can use provided information as-is, or you can use it to improve your own mockup process. Each chapter explains a different segment of that process, and provides concrete advice about commonly occurring situations I've encountered on many projects.

Part II is more loosely structured, and provides a broader context for all the advice from Part I. Two of the chapters describe real-life projects where mockups had an important role. The main value here are challenges that arose and how the teams have responded.

At the very end, I have compiled the take-aways from all the chapters. Readers have reported these take-aways useful by themselves, so they are all here in one place, easy to find and skim through.

Terminology: Mockups vs Wireframes

Today, there is much talk about the difference between mockups and wireframes. Simply put, you can visualize wireframes as rough (often black and white) sketches, and high-fidelity mockups as a precise design specification.

However, in this book I mostly use the word "mockup" for both mockups and wireframes, because it makes for easier reading and traditionally encompasses both terms.

Disclosure

Several people have pointed out that I need to make this point clear in advance. I'm the author of a commercial mockup tool, www.MockupScreens.com, which was created in 2004 and is still active and growing.

However, in this book, I don't promote or even mention (except in the tools chapter) my own mockup tool or any others. Instead, I focus on specific concepts and techniques that I believe my readers will find useful.

Acknowledgements

Many people have contributed to this book — thank you all! I'd especially like to thank Darko Marijančić for providing a tough critique of each version even as I was writing it, and Tomislav Uzelac for multiple rounds of merciless fluff-elimination and editing.

Help Your Customers Understand What They Are Going to Get

Software projects are notorious for new requirements that pop up in the middle of the project. If you're not careful, you can quickly find yourself shooting at a moving target.

Developers complain that customers don't know what they want, while customers complain that they have other things to do, rather than explaining and re-explaining the obvious.

Many years ago, a customer said something that finally resonated with me on the subject.

At the time, I was refusing to start the development process until the specification made sense to the customer. To that end, we were reviewing the latest

Shooting At a Moving Target

- New requirements often arise in the middle of the project.
- Developers complain that customers don't know what they want.
- Customers complain about having to explain the obvious.

version of the spec, and I was furious. I was trying to make everything perfect, but she simply wasn't cooperating. Marlene, the customer, was bored by the (quite technical) spec, and often didn't elaborate on the consequences of any changes that we made. They were obvious to her, after all, why would she even bring them up?

I finally complained about her attitude, only to be answered with "If I ordered the steak, I wouldn't have to ask for a knife."

We kept moving forward with the project, but I couldn't stop thinking about what she had said. Marlene was right, in a way. This approach wasn't working.

Traditional Approaches to Requirements

When capturing software requirements, you can either create a detailed specification up-front, or you can work in small iterations.

I inherited a detailed spec in the above example, but it wasn't particularly good. Developing a good specification is very time consuming.

> **Two Paths for Requirements**
>
> - Detailed specification up-front.
> - Working in short iterations.

In my situation, as the original spec had grown, the people involved became more and more reluctant to change anything. Small inconsistencies and discarded issues were building up, and if they were left 'as is', they would only explode in our faces later.

Marlene and I finally made some progress when I rebuilt the whole spec into use-cases and scenarios. It did make more sense to describe things from the user's point of view.

You should take into account that this was back in the year 2000. Design patterns were coming into fashion, while use-cases were just starting to be used by a wider audience. The concept of iterative development was beginning to push into the mainstream, and UML was seen as the new big hope for software development. There were plenty of new toys to experiment with.

Detailed Specification Up-Front

- Time consuming.
- Small inconsistencies build up over time.
- Resistant to changes.

Marlene and I finally came to understand one another, but it was still proving to be tedious work. Among other measures we tried, we decided to take an iterative approach.

Short iterations actually delivered what they were supposed to and they regularly uncovered issues that we had missed. These improvements were made in following iterations, and so the process went on for many months.

Short Development Iterations

- They uncover issues quickly.
- Possible improvements compete with deadlines.
- The contract must allow for iterations.

However, feelings were mixed. They ranged from relief to desperation, or even both at the same time. Obviously, it was immensely helpful to find any problems as early as possible, but that also meant that we would never be finished.

The contract simply hadn't accounted for this. Somehow, we had to perform this iteration approach more efficiently. It was time for another face-to-face talk.

A Picture is Worth a Thousand Words

Marlene insisted that she and her colleagues could not fully understand what they were going to get until they saw it. It came down to the ancient question of which came first, the chicken or the egg?

Fortunately, we found a loophole. Most of the problems that business people found wouldn't actually require a fully working application. A simple "picture" might actually be enough.

Figure 1.A: E-commerce website mockup

This is a text-only description for the above example. Although simplified, it's already getting too complex to clearly communicate the information.

Website header:
- Logo.
- The name "Sports Online Store".
- Options to login or create new account.

General functions:
- Search, it opens special version of item catalog.
- Change currency.
- Display number of items in the cart.
- Go to shopping cart.

Main navigation:
- Above the item catalog.
- Options to filter items for men, women or kids.
- Browse items by sport or brand.
- Main browsing categories.

Category navigation:
- Shows all subcategories
- Shows item types for current subcategory.
- Visitor can chose whole subcategory or item type.

Item catalog:
- Display number of items found.
- Allows sorting by price, date added or satisfaction.
- Default sort is by price, lowest first.
- Allows changing number of items shown, default is 20.
- Pagination.
- Shows items in a grid with item pictures, like a thumbnail gallery.

Single item in a gallery:
- Picture of the item, size is 150x150.
- Item name.
- Item price.
- Average number of "stars" left by reviewers.
- "Stars" are displayed graphically
- Total number of reviews left by customers.
- Click on an item opens its details.

Other:
- Link to Help is available.
- Page title: website name and the name of current page

Figure 1.B: E-commerce website textual description

So we switched to mockups. We continued with the iterative approach as before, but with mockups instead of code. Only when the people handling the business side had no further objections, did we start coding.

Short Mockup Iterations

- They uncover issues immediately.
- Requirements are agreed upon before the coding starts.

Our efficiency increased and the iterative approach finally made sense. When combined with using mockups instead of coding each iteration, the results were very good.

We quickly switched to the same approach for everything we did and we've never looked back.

Printable Take-Aways

Note that printable take-aways for all the chapters are available on this web-page:

http://www.mockups101.com/resources

Part I:
Creating and Using Mockups

CHAPTER 1

The Basic Mockup Routine

Mockups are easy to do, and everyone understands them. This doesn't mean that you'll be fine no matter what you do. I, for one, have made many costly oversights in the years since adopting this approach. With that in mind, I've created this guide to help you avoid the same mistakes in your own projects.

What I recommend is that you use a basic proven routine for your projects. However, there are several points I need you to understand first.

1.1 Mockups Can Be Done by Anyone.

Think about it. Mockups can be as simple as paper sketches. While I don't recommend sticking to pen and paper, this approach proves that you don't need any technical expertise to create mockups.

Several weeks back, my

Mockups Are Useful Because:

- They are easy to create.
- Everyone can understand them.
- Mockups can be made by anyone.

nine-year-old son talked me into developing a battle-card game together. To explain his idea, he drew an interface for the game, and he was quite adamant about what needed to be where and why.

It's exactly the same situation with your analysts or subject matter experts. With mockups, they can simply show you what they mean, rather than telling you and relying on and assuming a mutual understanding.

1.2 Reworking Mockups Is Cheap

Since mockups can be done many times faster than code, you don't need to stubbornly defend them. When there are flaws, you simply rework your mockups. It's so fast, you can even start from scratch when needed.

> **Mockups Are Created Quickly**
>
> - You can afford to throw mockups away at any time.
> - Reworking them repeatedly is perfectly acceptable.

Therefore, the logical strategy becomes using every shakedown opportunity you can. Instead of shrinking from objections, you actively encourage them until you make your prototype watertight.

1.3 Mockups Make It Easy to Engage Your Customers

Involving a customer early saves a ton of trouble, everyone tells you. That's all well and good, but it's far from easy to accomplish.

Instead of spending days writing documents that no one really wants to read, you can sketch the screens in a matter of hours and give your customer something that they will immediately understand.

> **Involve Your Customers Early**
>
> - With mockups, customers can show you precisely what they mean.
> - Mockups tend to make communication productive and down-to-earth.

Also, mockups tend to make communication productive and down-to-earth. Early in a project, this can be a great advantage.

1.4 The Basic Mockup Routine

Early on, the mockups are about the only thing that everyone can understand. However, just using the mockups is, by itself, no guarantee of success.

Mockups are just a communication device, so how you actually use your mockups to communicate is what's important.

The basic procedure of using mockups looks like this:

The Basic Mockup Routine:

1. **Sketch several related screens.**
   A good choice are steps a user takes to accomplish a task.

2. **Discuss them with the customer.**
   Discuss these sketches with your customer and annotate them. This is best done in live workshops.

3. **Flesh out the details.**
   Flesh out the details over several quick iterations. Don't try to get everything correct from the start.

4. **Repeat.**
   Repeat the same procedure for the next batch of screens.

Figure 2: The basic mockup routine

That being said, each step has its own traps, like creating wrong expectations, or getting the wrong kind of feedback. We'll come back to these after explaining the basic process in little more detail.

1.5 Several Related Screens Make a Digestible Package

Customers have very little time to take away from their everyday tasks. For that reason, lengthy documents terrify them, as well as anything even remotely technical.

On the other hand, three or four mockups at a time won't scare anyone and your customer will be genuinely curious about what you have come up with.

At this point, your main goal is to get your customers' attention and cooperation.

One obstacle at the beginning is getting everyone on the same page. It helps if the mockups that you discuss are related. This provides an immediate context for your customers to dive in - no explanations necessary.

Shopping Cart, Related Screens:	**Registration, Related Screens:**
• Shopping Cart • Shipping Options • Checkout • Confirmation • Thank You	• Create Account • Terms and Conditions • Preferences • Check Your E-mail • Sign In

Figure 3: How to group related screens

The best way to start is with several main screens of the application that you are developing. This way, your context is the big picture. Your customers will therefore share their opinions on the most important matters, for example if they recognize that you are not aware of some part of their business process.

Later on, you will want to switch the context to get more depth.

A good way to proceed is to focus on individual scenarios. This shows your customers how real people will eventually use the application, which will further attract their attention. It will also make their feedback productive and genuine.

Mock-up Several Related Screens:

- This will get your customers' attention.
- It provides an immediate business context.

Tip:

- Start with main business screens. Continue with scenarios.

Note that I use the word scenario here as a rather loose term. It can be a user story, or a use-case, or a number of other things. It doesn't really matter.

What does matter is to:

- Get and keep your customers' attention.

- Start with a big picture, and dive into details later.

1.6 Use On-Screen Annotations

You create the mockups, discuss them with your customer and diligently write down anything important that you discover, but where do you write it down?

Right there on the screen!

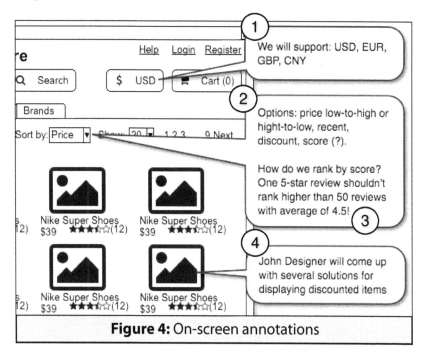

Figure 4: On-screen annotations

Four things are especially useful to put on your mockups as on-screen comments (see the anotations on Figure 4):

- When a decision is made (1).

- If there is a dilemma (2).

- When you have a question (3).

- Who will investigate an issue and report back (4).

As simple as it sounds, the implications are huge. When you make your annotations a visual part of the mockup, they become hard to miss and even harder to ignore.

1.7 Mockups Should Be Quick and Iterations Short

Iterations are a powerful concept. When it's hard to do the job perfectly in one go, it makes sense to do the first pass quickly, then assess what you have and tweak the results until the job is done.

However, iterations often require doing the same thing twice, or even several times. Can you afford that on software projects?

With mockups, you can. They are exponentially faster than coding, and so is any rework that proves

Mockups Work Well In Iterations:

- Mockups are exponentially faster than coding.
- They allow for very quick iterations.

to be required after assessing each iteration's results.

Thus, work in short iterations and plan them in advance:

- Schedule two workshops for each batch of mockups with your customer.

- Hold several rounds of less formal discussions between those two formal workshops.

The more iterations you make, the better the results will be. Fortunately, many ideas can be discussed by phone or email: "Here is a new version of that screen. Is it better now?" These are your micro-iterations.

You want to have as many of these as you need, so don't waste time on perfecting mockups for any single micro-iteration. Instead, focus on testing your ideas quickly and getting immediate feedback.

In other words, your iterations for a single batch of screens might look like this:

Iterations For One Batch of Mockups:

1. Formal workshop: discussing the initial mockups.
2. Micro-iterations:
   A. Getting feedback on mockups in progress.
   B. Getting feedback on mockups in progress.
   C. (...)
3. Formal workshop: presenting and confirming the mockups.

Figure 5: Mockup iterations example

CHAPTER 2

Make It Obvious That Mockups Are Not the Real Thing

At the beginning of a project, you need to make it clear your mockups are just that - work in progress.

Why it's so important? Because this single piece of advice will steer you clear of a whole set of irritating problems. What follows are clear examples of what can easily happen otherwise.

Common Problems

- False sense of progress.
- Too much design feedback.
- Confused developers.

2.1 Avoid False Sense of Progress

Too realistic mockups will create a false sense of progress, early on. Such mockups automatically translate into, "There's only some wiring under-the-hood left" in your customers' minds. After this happens, there is nothing much you can do: they have already seen it with their own eyes.

You need to make painfully clear that your screens are only mockups and not the real thing. Make this visually obvious, it's what people *see* that matters.

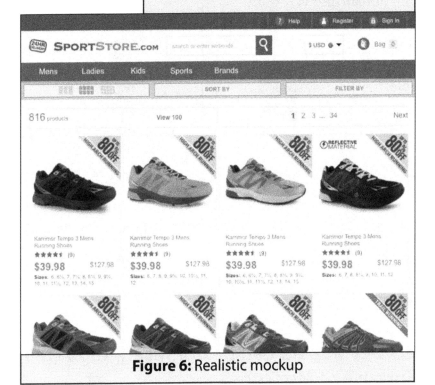

Figure 6: Realistic mockup

2.2 Don't Get Drowned in Design Feedback

If you present realistic mockups, you will get all kinds of design feedback - the kind that you typically don't want at this point in the process.

Early on in the project, you are struggling to agree on basic structure and functionality, so you want to avoid discussions on fonts, colors, and visual identity. Those discussions and objections are wasting time that both you and your customer don't have and can't afford.

Fonts, Color, Alignment, ...

- People will comment on what they see.
- Typically, you don't want this kind of feedback early on.

Mockups are useful because users comment primarily on what they see, so let them see exactly what you need them to comment on. You can switch to realistic screens later.

So far, we were only focusing on users, but you will also be communicating with developers, and they will likely present different surprises for you.

2.3 Developers Can Be Confused About the Purpose of Mockups

I was working on one project where a specification was needed extra fast, for a remote development team. Therefore, low-fidelity mockups were used to pin down the requirements, in order to provide the spec to developers on time. Mockups were attached as zipped HTML pages, with a note that they were only presented to illustrate the ideas explained in the spec.

In the first internal build, the system worked fine, but the user interface was both sub-standard and a surprise. GUI developers built upon the actual HTML code from the mockups.

The trouble didn't stop there. When contacted, the developers loudly complained that the HTML they had received was terrible, and that the people creating the mockups should have a better understanding of their framework's capabilities.

The idea that one might produce a code that wasn't intended for use simply had no place in those developers' universe. As a result, they disregarded the instructions without a second thought.

> **Developers Are Your Users Too**
>
> • Don't expect mutual understanding to come for free, you have to work on it.

Have you noticed the pattern here? Developers acted in exactly the same way users would. Without a dedicated "translator", they saw what they expected to see.

There are many ways that developers can misuse mockups, but the above example makes one thing painfully clear:

Developers are your users, too.

With that in mind, don't expect mutual understanding to come for free. You have to work on it, just as you do with your customers.

2.4 Use Black and White Mockups Early On

The above problems are common examples of what can easily happen in an apparently simple project. If you haven't paid attention to what exactly you are communicating *visually*, you'll have a hard time to undo any wrong impressions. Words are no match for images in this type of communication.

Fortunately, you can avoid these mistakes by simply being aware of them. Thus, what you do is *visually* communicate what you want your users to see.

First, you don't do "nice" mockups, at least not in the beginning. You can use pen and paper, or even a drawing board. Realistically though, you're better off with a specialized mockup tool that will allow you to easily make frequent changes. However, make sure to use a sketch-

Black and White Mockups

- They don't create false sense of progress.
- Such mockups won't evoke design feedback.
- They won't confuse your own team.

based appearance or a black-and-white look and feel that clearly shows it as a work-in-progress.

This way, you are communicating that mockups are only that – mockups. No one will confuse sketches for the real thing, neither your customers, nor your developers.

CHAPTER 3

Provoking the Right Feedback

You use mockups to clarify what your application is supposed to do. This sounds simple - you sketch some screens, show them to your customer, and then pass on the results to your developers. Usually, however, this is not enough.

Many times, you will not be getting the precise feedback that you need.

Often, your customer clams up when confronted with anything remotely technical. On the other hand, they might be eager to help, but simply don't understand what kind of feedback you require. In both situations, it is not enough to be a good listener.

It's Not Enough to Be a Good Listener

- You must actively provoke feedback.
- You need to target the right kind of feedback.

You must provoke feedback actively!

3.1 Populate Mockups with Realistic Data

If you present empty screens with no data, they won't ever be discussed in great detail. On the other hand, when you put real names and numbers there, you are magically triggering the customers' expertise.

Also, data should be chosen to specifically provoke a response. Any time that you have doubts about something, put it right there on the screen. If you can't decide between two choices, put the controversial one in the spotlight.

Just compare the following examples: one is an empty mockup and the other is populated with data. You'll see immediately what I'm talking about.

> ## Empty Screens Don't Encourage Discussion
>
> - Realistic data is what triggers the customers' expertise.
> - Data should be chosen to provoke a response.
> - Put the questionable choices in the spotlight.

Empty screen such as this states only the obvious. As a consequence, any issues will be uncovered only later.

| Register | X |

Sports Online Store

Help   Login   Register

Registration

* E-mail address: [_____]

* First name: [_____]

* Last name: [_____]

* Date of birth: [_____]

* Country: [_____]

* Address: [_____]
[_____]

* Town: [_____]

* State: [_____]

* Postal code: [_____]

* Phone: [_____]

* Password: [_____]

* Confirm password: [_____]

* Indicates required fields

[Register]

Figure 7.A: Empty-screen mockup

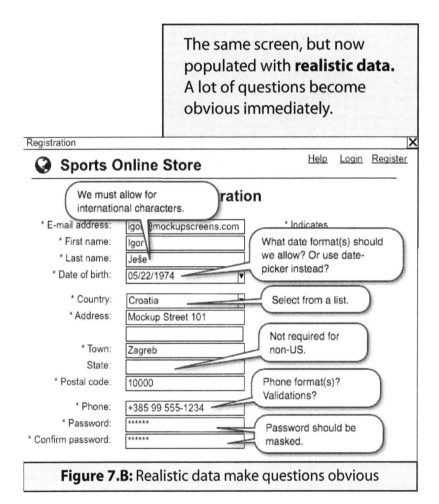

The same screen, but now populated with **realistic data.** A lot of questions become obvious immediately.

Registration ☒

🌐 **Sports Online Store** Help Login Register

We must allow for international characters. ration

* Indicates

* E-mail address: igor@mockupscreens.com
* First name: Igor
* Last name: Ješe
* Date of birth: 05/22/1974

What date format(s) should we allow? Or use date-picker instead?

* Country: Croatia

Select from a list.

* Address: Mockup Street 101

Not required for non-US.

* Town: Zagreb
State:
* Postal code: 10000

Phone format(s)? Validations?

* Phone: +385 99 555-1234
* Password: ******
* Confirm password: ******

Password should be masked.

Figure 7.B: Realistic data make questions obvious

34

3.2 Put the Issues in the Spotlight

While you struggle to understand your customer's needs, you always have plenty of questions. Asking will get you some answers, but harder decisions often tend to be left for later. Especially if there are alternatives your customers either don't fully understand or can't agree on among themselves.

What you can do, is to make an initial choice yourself, as a baseline for assessing the alternatives. Integrating one specific choice into the screens will demonstrate it's consequences and trigger a discussion. That way, no one will be able to postpone or ignore any decisions that need to be made.

Can integrating such choice and its ramifications into your screens be too much work? Sometimes it can. The alternative approach is to note the question right there on the mockup. Or if you have a recommendation, write that on the screen instead.

Issues Can Be Ignored, Consequences Can't

- Typically, people won't rush to answer questions.
- Instead, put the repercussions in the spotlight.
- If those bother someone, they usually won't hesitate to tell you so.

For example, "Vendors are sorted by most recent orders on top. Search function is NOT needed." Put this as a visual comment, so people won't be shy to express their opinions.

When your customer is commenting on "the screens", he will criticize the presence of these visual notes - very directly, if you did it right.

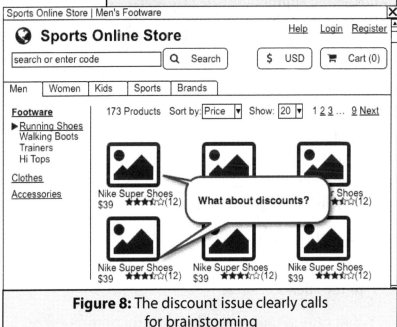

> When faced with a choice of options, present the one most likely to **provoke discussion.** Business people will typically jump right in, and tell you whether something won't work.

Figure 8: The discount issue clearly calls for brainstorming

3.3 Group Screens to Provide Business Context

When eliciting feedback, you want your customer's expertise, everything else is secondary. The question is how do you get them into the expert mindset right from the start?

One approach that works is to organize the mockups into scenarios. Sketching each step of the scenario might look like overkill, but it's actually quite easy. You copy and paste the appropriate screen, and then change the data to reflect each step. Mock-up important exceptions as well, while you're at it.

Any batch of tightly related screens will do the job, but scenarios result in several extra benefits:

> ### Related Screens Provide Business Context
>
> - Any batch of tightly related screens will work.
> - Scenarios are a good choice: they are quick and easy to create, and they test your own understanding.

- They are quick and easy to create.

- They test your own understanding before presenting it to the clients or users.

- You can't get more detailed than this, process-wise.

Once you have your scenario fleshed out, lead your customer through each step. Wherever you think there might be a problem, spell it out for the audience. Leave enough of a pause, and someone will inevitably jump in.

Note that the advice presented in this chapter is not a collection of tricks, or aimed at manipulating your customer. It's the exact opposite. In fact, these are very basic and common communication techniques that can be very useful when tweaked for this particular context and have proven their value over time. Remember to use them when they are called for and you will get the benefits.

Provoking the Right Feedback, Summarized

- Populate mockups with realistic data.
- Put the issues in the spotlight.
- Group screens to provide business context.

As these techniques are tailored specifically to elicit feedback, others will help you to discuss the mockups more effectively, as explained in the next chapter.

CHAPTER 4

Discussing the Mockups Effectively

Mockups are great for communicating with your customer, and there are numerous ways you can use them for that purpose. You can, for example, send them via email as images or attached as PDF files. This might even be the only option when your customer is thousands of miles away.

However, it's better to present mockups in live workshops whenever possible.

With this method, you can tweak the mockups right there in the meeting. Then, even your on-screen notes become the result of a joint effort. This single point can make a difference between success and failure later, when tough decisions need to be defended.

> **Present Mockups In Live Workshops When Possible**
>
> - You can tweak the mockups right there in the meeting.
> - Mockups and on-screen notes become the result of collaboration.

Keep all of that in mind, whether you are conducting live workshops or not. There are two important points to begin with:

1. Screens should be populated with realistic data and chosen specifically to provoke feedback.

2. In early workshops, you should exclusively use black-and-white (or sketched) mockups. You will be switching to a more realistic look and feel later on in the process.

4.1 Test Your Own Understanding

In live workshops, present your ideas for each screen: what a particular element means and why it's there, as well as what happens when a user clicks a button, etc.

Determine where each piece of data comes from. For example, if the table has a "Date" column, specify which date it is exactly: a creation date, date of the last update, or something entirely different. Pay special attention to data that has to be calculated or comes from other systems.

Test Your Ideas For Each Screen

- What a particular element means?
- Why is it there?
- Where does each piece of data come from?
- Is there any calculated data or data from other systems?

What you are actually doing is searching for any holes in your system. All the details you get will be a welcome byproduct early on. Later, when you need to focus on these issues, you will already have nailed quite a lot of them.

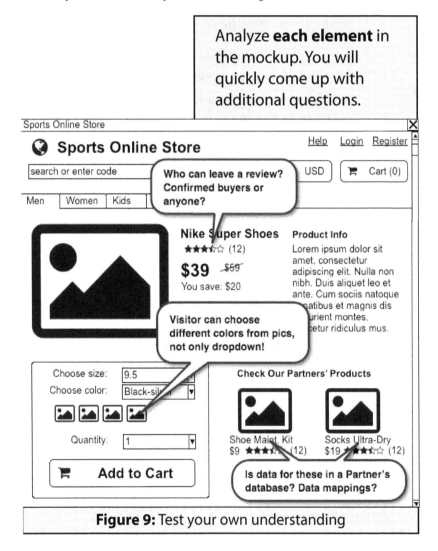

Figure 9: Test your own understanding

Above all, be prepared to listen. Your goal is to get the feedback, so when your customers have something to say, let them do the talking. Feel free to moderate enough to stay on topic though. Steering the conversation back to the mockups is often perfectly enough to get back on track.

4.2 How to Avoid Non-Productive Discussions

Everyone has attended a meeting that at some point seemed to go in circles. Don't allow your workshops to go down that road. Sometimes you'll need to break or end non-productive discussions.

This might not seem like an easy thing to avoid, especially if you deal with high-ranking people having a great deal of self-importance, who also happen to be signing your checks.

Fortunately, there is a safe and established way out of these frustrating situations.

Simply agree on something, such as, "There are several possibilities here. These

How to Escape Non-Productive Discussions

1. Agree that the issue does exist.
2. Assign someone to investigate and make that an on-screen note.
3. Move on to the next topic.

specific people will investigate them and then distribute the results". Make that delegation into an on-screen note, which should satisfy a person that is potentially derailing your workshop. Then, matter-of-factly switch to the next topic.

In this way, you can cover a vast number of potential issues (which is usually the case in the beginning), and do it all in a relatively short meeting.

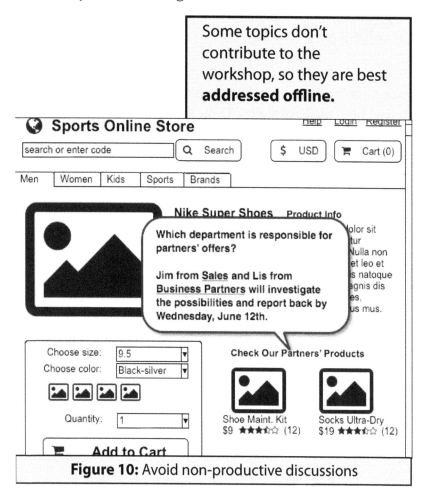

Figure 10: Avoid non-productive discussions

4.3 Make Your Customers Care

In these types of workshops, don't be afraid to tweak mockups together with your customer. Most times, they will love the effort. More importantly, you are producing the result together, which makes your customers care too!

Tweak Mockups Together With Your Customers
• They will appreciate the effort.
• You are producing the result together, so it makes them care too!

If they feel invested in the project, they will work hard to understand your spec, care for it, and defend it when the need arises.

4.4 Create Opportunities for More Tests

With some preparation, after a number of iterations, you'll get to the no-objections point. Testing your own understanding definitely will have proved its worth, and uncovered critical issues that would otherwise only surface much later.

Why not push a bit further along these same lines?

One way to find opportunities for more tests is to mock-up system *outputs*: reports, exports, and similar items, as explained in the following chapter.

CHAPTER 5

Mocking-Up the Outputs

Most often, your system's main purpose is to produce specific outputs. While your mockups might be rough and approximate for the early stages, it's essential that they should be detailed for the visible *results* that your customer is paying for.

It's not simply about meeting your users' concerns either. Each element of every output needs to be provided by the system. You can help yourself investigating these situations by creating mock outputs.

Note that mocking-up the outputs has no additional cost for you, because you would need to detail them anyway.

Mock Outputs Need to Be Detailed

- Each element needs to come from somewhere.
- Required data needs to exist.
- A specific part of the system is responsible.

5.1 Mock Outputs Need to Be Detailed

What's the best time to start? Usually not from Day One, but do it as soon as you have a decent understanding of the system.

When you do create *detailed* word-by-word mockups for the outputs, then:

- If it's a screen, refine your existing mockup.

- If it's a report, great. Create a mockup in Word.

- When it's a table, do it in Excel.

If it's in any other format, you should still consider Word or Excel first; this way, you can let your users clarify things among themselves. It's their business process, after all.

Use Tools that Your Customers Are Comfortable With

- If it's a report, then use MS Word.
- For tables, use Excel.

Tip:

- This allows your customers to clarify details among themselves.

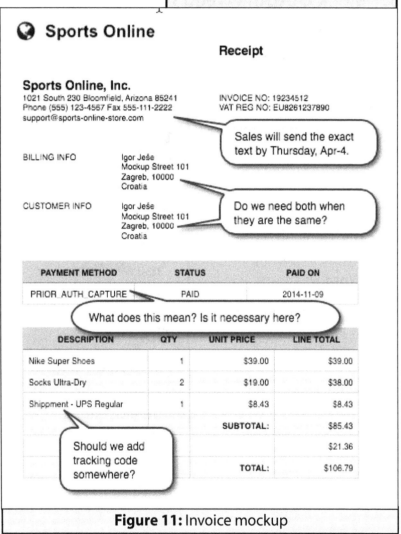

Figure 11: Invoice mockup

5.2 Be Precise With the Data

For all of these steps, using realistic data is critical, so obtain a relevant sample of real data for your examples. It will come handy for other activities too.

If realistic data doesn't exist, the first order of business is to make it up. However, you need to make it logically consistent across different parts of the system; therefore, it's best to do this together with your customer.

Now, any piece of data must come from somewhere — this is why you cannot rely on approximations here. Take a report, for example; what data does it contain exactly? Where does each piece of data come from? If it's a calculation, where is the algorithm?

Prepare a Relevant Sample of Realistic Data

- It should be logically consistent across different parts of the system.
- Involve your customer in obtaining the data.

Tip:

- Such data sample is very useful for development, testing, etc.

5.3 Cross-Check It in the Opposite Direction

This goes the other way around as well: no part of the system exists without doing something. However silly this may sound, sometimes you just can't see that a part of your system produces any visible results.

Investigate it, you might have missed a report or some small detail that will make all the difference.

> **No Part of the System Exists Without Doing Something**
>
> • A part of your system doesn't produce any visible results?
> • If so, you might have missed an output, such as a report.

5.4 When Are the Mockups Done?

By now, you should have quite a lot:

- "No-objection" mockups for scenarios of real-life use.

- Reports and other outputs specified in detail, made together with your customer.

- A set of realistic data to use for preliminary testing, etc.

- Your accompanying notes. These cover anything of importance that has come up throughout the course of the process.

When you have all of these, your mockups have done their job. Your developers definitely don't have to rely on guesswork; instead, they have high-quality inputs that they can understand immediately.

Mocked Outputs, Summarized

- Outputs need to be detailed.
- Prepare a relevant sample of realistic data to work with.

Part 2:
Putting It All Together

CHAPTER 6

Mockups as a Spec

Good mockups accurately describe system behavior and its outputs. However, screen sketches by themselves don't constitute a specification. There are additional details that developers need to know. For example, system constraints and other non-functional requirements are important, as well as exact algorithms and calculations.

> ## Screen Sketches Are Not Enough
>
> - Developers need a complete and accurate representation of the system.
> - Develop your notes in parallel with your mockups. You will need them to connect all the dots.

What your developers need from you is the complete and accurate representation of the system, both in terms of its function and its behavior.

With that in mind, go through all of your mockups and notes in order to assess what you have. Then, add the information from another important source: your own solid understanding of the system and its details.

There is a quick way to connect all the dots at this point. I call it the "Diverge-Converge" approach:

1. Diverge: Quickly write down everything not covered by your mockups or your notes, without thinking about form or structure.

2. Converge: Structure and compile all the information together, filling the gaps as you go.

6.1 Diverge: Find the Gaps

First, you methodically go through everything you have accumulated - every screen and every note, one by one. As you examine each of them, various thoughts on those ideas or issues will likely jump out anyway, so write them down. This requires no order and no structure. Just write everything down as fast as you can.

Diverge

- Quickly write down everything not covered by your mockups or your notes.
- Don't worry about form or structure.
- Quick bullets are a good way to do it.

Why not structure or analyze the information? Because you need to keep your thoughts flowing without stopping or becoming distracted. This way, you will be able to do this first pass far more rapidly and pour out more information at one time.

6.2 Converge: Compile the Information

When you have finished "emptying your head", the resulting mess of information might not look very nice. However, you will be surprised at the sheer quantity of information that you have poured out.

Now, export your mockups to your favorite word processor, compile all the info into a spec, structure everything and present it logically.

Please don't add anything that doesn't improve the information. I have lost count of how many times I have seen a genuinely priceless piece of information polluted with piles of useless fluff.

This excess is usually used for the sake of completeness or to adhere

> ### Compiling the Information
>
> - The "Diverge" step typically leaves you with a huge amount of information.
> - You need to structure everything and present it logically.
> - Don't try to cram everything into on-screen notes. Use a word-processor instead.

to company templates. If you positively must do it, try to separate all the extraneous material into appendices.

Keep your main document light and clean. This way, you are actually encouraging people to read it.

When you are ready, present the spec in person (as opposed to sending it by email) to your customer for final confirmation.

This step is crucial, and this sort of presentation only takes a few hours. Even a teleconference is far superior to giving your customer a pile of papers to sign off on, or an impersonal email for them to review.

Now, all of this information sums up this process in an ideal world. For most projects, everything mentioned can be done in a relatively short time.

> **Brevity Encourages People to Read Your Spec**
>
> - Keep your main document light and clean.
> - Eliminate anything that doesn't improve the information.
> - Separate all the extraneous material into appendices.

The whole procedure explained above, from first mockups to the compilation of all the information, has evolved throughout the course of many projects with that precise goal in mind.

6.3 The Alternative: the Fireman's Approach

Sometimes you can't afford to go for an accurate and complete spec. Perhaps you were called in only after developers realized that the spec was not up to par. Maybe deadlines were so menacing that everything blurred into a mad dash of overlapping activities that were difficult to organize or record appropriately.

When you find yourself between a rock and a hard place, even rough mockups are better than nothing. These are better when presented with a generous amount of on-screen notes, especially in such complex situations. This way, exporting your mockups into a .doc or .pdf will give you something-like-a-spec in no time.

Getting Results in Shortest Time Possible

- In a crisis, even rough mockups can make a difference.
- Make plenty of on-screen notes.
- Keep one-step ahead of developers and always be available.
- Have your customers dedicate people for you.

Using this approach, each screen is likely to have **dozens of notes.**

1.	Entering product code directly opens product details.
2.	Currencies supported: USD, EUR, GBP, CNY.
3.	Cart button shows a number of items already in the cart.
4.	Help is opened in another window/tab.
5.	When a customer is already logged-in, customer's username is shown instead of Login/Register. A click on it opens customer's profile.
6.	We need another main tab: "Deals". It has to be visually different from five main categories.
7.	Product's picture can be rotated by dragging.
8.	Click on the picture opens a big picture as an overlay dialog.
9.	One of product pictures need to be designated as default in back-end.
10.	Stars icons are either full-star, half-star, or empty star.
11.	Number of reviews includes only confirmed buyers.
12.	Not every product has a discounted price.
13.	Product info can be 200 characters long. If it's longer, full info shows in an on-hover pop-up.
14.	"Choose size" offers only available sizes.
15.	"Choose color" offers only available colors.
16.	Additional pics show only available colors. A click on one chooses that color and changes the main pic.
17.	Quantity cannot offer more items than available on stock.

Figure 12: Using notes instead of a formal spec

In that case however, be prepared for some significant multi-tasking for yourself.

Be available.

You will need to clarify each tiny detail for your developers as you go along, especially the workings "under the hood".

Keep one-step ahead of development.

You can't do everything at once, so you will be doing quite a lot of triage. For modules that need to enter development, tweak the rough mockups until they are confirmed. For modules that are already in development, focus on detailing the main outputs.

At the very least, plan to start early in order to give your customer time to decide on any ambiguities in the business process.

Keep One Step Ahead of Developers

- For modules that need to enter development, tweak the rough mockups until they are confirmed.
- For modules that are already being developed, focus on detailing the main outputs.

Since you have two simultaneous goals here, it's strongly suggested to have two people (or teams of two people each) on this. One person should focus on the workflow (rough mockups), and the other on the outputs.

Have your customer dedicate people for this.

Needless to say, fast and functional communication with your customer is a must. Insist that the customer dedicates people to help you and that they have the appropriate authority.

In short, mockups can also work as a spec if you have no other option or don't mind living on the edge.

An Ideal Customer Representative:

- Has significant operational hands-on experience.
- Has enough authority and initiative to make quick design decisions.

CHAPTER 7

Real World Case Studies

In real life situations, you want to avoid looking for the best way to do things. Instead, use what you understand. Also, everything you do should be for a clear and specific purpose.

Mockups can save you tons of time and effort, but you have to use them in a way that is meaningful for the circumstances. If you feel your process doesn't work on a particular project, then change it.

Let me give you some real life examples of project decisions, along with their reasoning and respective consequences.

There Is No Single Best Way

- Use what you understand.
- Everything should have a clear and specific purpose.
- When a process doesn't work for you, adjust it accordingly.

7.1 Case Study No.1: Brand New Workflows, Tight Deadlines

This was a moderately big system for the government. New regulations resulted in new workflows that needed to be automated.

It was nothing special, technically speaking, but new workflows are always a challenge.

Up to this point, users haven't actually tried out these new workflows in real life. They had some idea how the new processes should work, but they still didn't grasp new processes as well as old workflows.

Immediate Challenges

- New workflows were not fully understood.
- Lead-time has been wasted on the process itself.

Another problem was the deadline. Lead-time had been wasted on the project process itself.

Months had gone by in producing all kinds of required architectural documents, which had to be approved and signed off by experts. This despite the fact that both hardware and software architectures were well established and already in production. Go figure.

When requirement analysis finally started, developers were already quite nervous, to put it mildly.

On a project of this size, any ambiguity in the overall specs was simply not acceptable. Discovering new exceptions or side-scenarios later on would make the whole project slip.

We needed a way to both determine and optimize the non-existing process, so we decided to use mockups as a simulation, instead of the typical proof-of-concept mockups.

Challenge: Workflows were completely new and therefore not well understood.

Response: The mockup process won't stop at proof-of-concept stage, but will instead go for a full simulation of the system.

We would actually simulate each new process, step-by-step, until every detail was sufficiently covered and until we felt that surprises were no longer possible.

Did I mention that we needed these mockups quickly?

Dedicated representatives expedited things *a lot*. Because of the deadline, we approached the customer and explained the situation. We requested two dedicated representatives. The first person was one of their operational hands-on workers. For the other representative, we needed someone with enough authority and initiative to make quick design decisions.

The discussion was rather tough, and the customer became more concerned by the minute, as you can imagine, but it worked.

> **Challenge:** Deadlines were tight.
>
> **Response:** Customers' representatives actively participated in mockup development.

I still can't decide whether the customer was just sufficiently scared by our actual presentation, or was the smartest person that I have ever met. We got the best two people they had, that were able to fill the exact roles that we needed.

Twenty frantic days followed. We were creating mockups and testing new ideas as quickly as we were discarding those that didn't work out.

> **Challenge:** We needed to quickly test alternative ideas and establish what approach would work best.
>
> **Response:** We did mockups in rapid micro-iterations.

First, we needed to pin down the workflows reasonably well. We did a huge number of quick-and-dirty sketches, attacking the workflows from every angle that we could think of and then rebuilding the workflows from scratch when needed, which happened more than a few times.

After several exhausting days, we finally felt that no more big surprises were left, so we moved on.

The system turned out to be very heavy in terms of data entry. Hundreds of data fields needed to be defined, along with syntactical checks for each, and logical validations and cross-validations for too many of them. Effectively grouping the data started to look like something that would make or break the project.

In response, we organized the work into two tracks. One track needed to specify each workflow in detail, while the other had to define the dataset that it required.

Challenge: We needed to be able to start from scratch when new realizations required it.

Response: We focused on one workflow at a time, starting with "quick and dirty" mockups.

We teamed up the customer operations guy with one of the analysts. They painstakingly identified each data field and investigated it, discovering and documenting where it came from and how it needed to be validated.

The rest of us were mocking up the complete screens and output documents for each workflow. Mockups started to take the shape of recognizable application screens.

To simulate each scenario, we needed real case data. We didn't have any, so we created a number of fake ones on paper, with proper case sleeves that contained a small pile of documents in each.

We ensured that each of several case types was covered. For each type, there was one case that represented a happy-day scenario, and several cases that covered all the relevant exceptions that we discovered.

Challenge: We needed to be able to test each workflow end-to-end, before the coding even started.

Response: Detailed and realistic mock data sets were created, including paper inputs, reports, printouts, etc.

It demonstrated that with a realistic case in your hands, everyone's understanding improved a lot, the customers' experts included.

We tested each workflow with everything mocked-up, including application screens, input paper documents, output paper documents, and output electronic reports. The issues were solved by tweaking and rebuilding the mockups before a single line of code was written.

When we were confident that the workflow was watertight, we simply handed the mockups and our notes to developers. Although the notes were on the heavy side, developers still had to ask for clarifications quite often.

Challenge: Developers had a lot of additional questions.

Response: An analyst was attached to developers full-time to elaborate on the mockups when needed.

We didn't have a traditional spec, remember, only the mockups and our notes. Therefore, we reassigned one analyst to work exclusively with the development team.

The results of this streamlined approach?

Developers were able to crank out the software in no time, and the system received almost no complaints in its first year of use.

That apparent success is all well and good, but let's get back to how we actually managed to pull it off.

- First, we decided on the appropriate strategy for the situation (full simulation with mockups) and pushed it through.

- Next, we aggressively prototyped the high-level requirements. We did it in micro-iterations, a half-day each or so. We didn't polish it to perfection, but moved on as soon as it was good enough.

- Only then did we mock-up everything. From paper documents to data validation errors, we actually tested the whole system with mockups, documenting everything as we went along.

It was hard work, of course, but it worked perfectly.

Challenge	Response
Workflows were completely new and therefore not well understood.	The mockup process won't stop at "proof-of-concept" stage, but will instead go for a full simulation of the system.
Deadlines were tight.	Customers' representatives actively participated in mockup development.
We needed to quickly test alternative ideas and establish what approach would work best.	Mockups were done in rapid micro-iterations.
We needed to be able to start from scratch when new realizations required it.	We focused on one workflow at a time, starting with "quick and dirty" mockups.
We needed to be able to test each workflow end-to-end, before the coding even started.	Detailed and realistic mock data sets were created, including paper inputs, reports, printouts, etc.
We didn't have the resources to develop a traditional specification.	Mockups were heavily annotated, to provide as much detail as feasible.
Developers had a lot of additional questions.	An analyst was attached to developers full-time, to elaborate on the mockups when needed.

Figure 13: Effectively using mockups on Project no.1

7.2 Case Study No.2: User Guide before Coding

Did you know that a User Manual can be a functional spec? Indeed, it can be a specification and a mockup at the same time.

This project had quite normal deadlines - not too relaxed, but comfortable enough. It was also relatively small, so we achieved workable communication quickly, which proved invaluable for tackling our first big challenge.

Initial Challenges

- Project objectives were entangled with out-of-scope issues.
- Very limited budget

This company had a number of existing problems in the business process that we were required to automate and not a big enough budget to solve them all. Thus, we had to be extremely careful in managing expectations.

We decided to write a very short project summary and clear it with the customers' top-level executive in person. The summary explained what problems this project was going to solve and listed the problems that were to be left for some future project to tackle.

I asked this executive to read it, a whole half-page, and promised him it was the only document I would require him to read. He gave me the look, but agreed. We quickly settled on several changes to the exact wording and that was it.

Why was this so important?

This was essential because during project kick-off, this modest half-page of text was projected on the wall first. I read it word-for-word and gave credit for it to the executive, who was standing and nodding thoughtfully right beside me.

Challenge: Project objectives were entangled with out-of-scope issues.

Response: Process (mockups) and scope limitations were backed by the customers' top-level executive.

Later on, people periodically tried to push for things that were not strictly in the project scope. What we simply said in response to that was "I understand you completely, but your executive explicitly said that this was not to be a part of this project." No one tried to get around that kind of argument.

There was another real challenge, however: the budget was quite thin, both at that moment and in the foreseeable future. There was little margin for rework.

Furthermore, the customer needed this system to serve about forty of their biggest clients, some of whom were accustomed to requesting customizations and getting their way.

The danger was that once the system went live, we could face a lot of additional requests, but there would be no budget for another round of development.

We had to give those big clients a chance to have their say, which we weren't sure how to do. Who should we include? Should we choose the biggest, the loudest, or the most loyal? Those left out could get irritated or downright angry.

Together with the customer, we decided to hold a client conference and present the new system to all forty of them. However, we would do that before the coding even started.

Challenge: Very limited budget.

Response: The entire system was mocked-up and tested. We included important end users.

We mocked-up the whole system and tested it with real-life documents and cases (with names and addresses changed), until both the customer and the developers agreed on what would work. Then, we started to prepare for the conference.

The question was how would we present the system to the clients? We needed to get feedback right there, in that meeting, without weeks of follow-up correspondence. Frankly, the specific goal was to give big clients a chance to voice their opinion, so that they wouldn't feel the need to do that later. To get any meaningful feedback, however, we needed to present the whole system, focus on the details that had the most importance for clients, and allow for ample discussion time on the conference agenda.

Challenge: How to effectively communicate detailed solution to end users.

Response: Mockups were turned into a User Guide. The Guide was organized into meaningful business scenarios displaying realistic data.

We decided to present a User Guide, prepared in a precise way to further the above goals more effectively:

- The User Guide would be organized into scenarios that had real business meaning for clients.

- A mockup would be shown for each important step, as well as each important exception.

- Mockups would contain real data.

- Under each mockup, each particular step would be explained.

- Below that explanation, all relevant business rules and data validations would be listed.

We got to work, and for once, it proved to come together surprisingly fast. We already had all the screens mocked-up, and all scenarios and exceptions were written down, along with related business rules and data validations. Thus, the only real work was writing the explanations for each step. We were lucky, however, to have just the right person for the job. She performed her tasks effortlessly and in mere days, our User Guide was polished and ready.

The most demanding users were asked to volunteer and help us.

We covertly showed the User Guide to some of the most demanding clients in advance. We justified it by asking them to volunteer to help us out with some details. As expected, they jumped at the opportunity to be the first commenters on the new system.

Challenge: Main clients were accustomed to requesting customizations.

Response: We involved main clients in the final iterations, by asking them to volunteer.

They made plenty of suggestions, and some of them were quite good. We acknowledged the important ones, which made them very happy, increasing their prestige among peers.

The conference itself took the whole day, albeit with plenty of coffee breaks to encourage discussions. A good lunch was arranged before the allotted time for discussion to sedate the most insistent people, just in case.

Every person attending received a hard copy of the User Guide and was encouraged to ask questions and write down notes, but the audience was asked to hold their full discussion until the allotted time.

The first part of the conference was the only time that I personally experienced the phenomena that I had witnessed so often: after we presented scenario after scenario, we had half convinced ourselves that these were not only mockups, but also a live system. The clients had no doubt at all.

Challenge: Accepting late feedback was not possible.

Response: User Conference was focused on promoting the solution and getting immediate feedback.

To be fair, we pointed out that it was only a design several times, and informed them that the system was still being developed. All of which was quite true, although a little exaggerated, considering that coding hadn't even started yet.

There were plenty of suggestions, and again, some were quite good. Most importantly, however, all of the suggestions were constructive and came from a place of good will. Those highly demanding clients had already perceived the system as their own baby; they had become involved before everyone else, after all.

After the conference, we implemented some of the changes that made the most sense. We also took care to include a number of suggested "cosmetic" changes just to demonstrate that we had been listening.

> **Challenge:** Demonstrating good will without accepting late changes.
>
> **Response:** The most important feedback was accepted along with a number of cosmetic changes.

Then, we simply gave the two documents to our developers. The User Guide was one, of course, and the other was the Technical Design, which were prepared and partly implemented in parallel.

Developers had no problems in implementing the system. First, the functional specifications were precise and quite mature. Secondly, developers were also at the conference, learning firsthand what problems and questions were arising from consumers and other industry professionals.

Developers understood the system before they saw the documentation.

They not only understood the system, but the whole picture.

User Acceptance was eminently simple. After all, customers personally created a baseline document together with us — the User Guide. User acceptance tests simply demonstrated that the system follows the User Guide to the letter, using the same scenarios, same exceptions, and the same dataset.

Both customer and developers had acceptance document from the start.

Challenge: User acceptance.

Response: User acceptance was based on the User Guide and mock documents and cases used from the start.

This was an interesting project to be a part of, as we took mockups to a completely new level:

- We based the User Guide on screen mockups.

- Iterations themselves became wider and wider audience-wise. The final (mockups) iteration de facto included virtually everyone affected by the system.

- The system was logically finished before the coding had even started.

Challenge	Response
Project objectives entangled with out-of-scope issues.	Process (mockups) and scope limitations were backed by the customer's top-level executive.
Very limited budget.	The entire system was mocked-up and tested, including mock documents and cases. Developers were included in this process.
How to communicate detailed solution to end users.	Mockups were turned into a User Guide. The Guide was organized into meaningful business scenarios displaying real data, including each step and important exceptions.
Main clients were accustomed to requesting customizations.	We involved main clients in the final iterations, asking them to volunteer.
Accepting late feedback was not possible.	We held a User Conference focused on getting immediate feedback.
Demonstrating good will without accepting late changes.	During iterations with clients and in the User Conference itself, the most important feedback was accepted along with a number of cosmetic changes.
Clear understanding with the developers.	Developers were expected to follow the User Guide, which they understood: they were involved in mockup iterations, and they attended the User Conference.
User acceptance.	User acceptance was based on the User Guide and mock documents and cases used from the start.

Figure 14: Effectively using mockups on Project no.2

7.3 Summing It All Up

There are numerous ways that mockups can help you. The most important lesson from the above examples is:

Mockups need a quick turnaround to be effective.

For that to work, you really need to start "light" with both your process and your documentation.

That way, you will be allowed to change a small batch of mockups over and over again until everyone agrees on them. Only then should you move on to more in-depth aspects, because less details means that changes are easier to make.

> ## Summing It All Up:
>
> - Mockups need a quick turnaround to be effective.
> - Use realistic scenarios and data whenever you can
> - Involve your customer from the very start.

Use real-life scenarios and data whenever you can.

Another important tactic is using real-life scenarios with real-life data. This greatly improves feedback, and allows for the testing of your mockups against real-life situations. The bonus in this approach is that you get test scenarios and test data for free, at least for the developers' testing and user acceptance tests.

Involve your customer from the very start.

It should be common knowledge that you need to involve your customer actively from day one. Everyone agrees on this, in theory, but during actual projects, I have heard many arguments against it, usually deteriorating into "us and them" attitude. Don't make this mistake, as it simply isn't true. Being surrounded by people equals communication. You better get good at it. Everything else is just an excuse.

I hope the above examples gave you an idea or two that you can use right away. Or, if you don't use mockups already, perhaps I persuaded you to try it on your next project. After all, only several years ago, creating mockups was considered more of an "alternative" approach. By now, however, it has become obvious that mockups greatly improve communication among all parties on a project, so mockups and/or wireframes are quickly gaining popularity in more mainstream applications.

CHAPTER 8

A Cautionary Tale

When you start with "light" documentation and quick mockup iterations, you can change your mockups until everyone agrees on them. Less details means that making changes is a lot easier, even starting from scratch may be acceptable.

The opposite happens if changes become virtually impossible from the start, which is usually justified as, "Why not do it right from the get-go?" More details cause changes within the cascade, as both your mockups and your documents gradually become impossible to update.

What follows is a different type of a case study, you might call it anti-patterns, if you like.

8.1 Ineffective Use of Mockups: Big Government Project, Process Paralysis

For this project, a large government agency hired a big consulting company, which would coordinate with three big IT companies to solve the problem for a completely different government agency. Thus, each of the two government agencies established its own ad-hoc body of subject matter experts to ensure the highest quality of results.

Both bodies were then joined into a single supervising committee, with several managers attached for good measure. Furthermore, neither of the companies wanted to be left out, so the companies pushed until their own experts were also admitted.

Immediate Challenges

- Convoluted organizational structure.
- Highly formal and complex process.

Months passed in the meeting stage over deciding on the right project organization. Then, discussions continued on appropriate methodologies to use, and on proper ways to use them. Compromises were made and process agreed upon.

It was decided that mockups were to be used, which would be done in three stages.

First, mockups were to be properly designed by mapping the actions from OOAD (Object-Oriented Analysis and

Design) and sequence diagrams, the UX (User Experience) diagrams were made with user interface logical objects and content bundles identified, grouped, and normalized.

Designs were then peer-reviewed and tested before being signed off. Testing was static, which basically meant that every minute detail had to be matched back to its related counterpart in all relevant design models, and vice versa.

Anti-Pattern

Mockups were not used early. Instead, they were only one of many outputs of a very formal analysis & design process.

Finally, the actual screens were drawn. They were incorporated into highly formal Use Cases, already halfway produced, which were presented to users in formal monthly workshops. Users were required to express their complaints in written form within a week.

Feedback opportunities were intentionally limited.

Someone finally figured out that time was slipping by, so those workshops started to double as requirements/ acceptance meetings.

This shift proved to be a bad decision. Customers simply couldn't be convinced to even try to understand the use-cases, all of which were highly formal and each approximately 30 pages in length. Nothing was omitted, regardless of how small it was, and countless tables describing data attributes and such were included.

There were almost one hundred use-cases in the model, some with a dozen alternative scenarios. You get the picture.

When customers had some feedback, it was usually about the mockups. However, any

Anti-Pattern

Mockups were not created in quick iterations to obtain early feedback. Instead, they were presented monthly and feedback was discouraged.

change in the mockups also meant changing the sequence diagrams, component diagrams, operational model, UX diagrams, traceability matrices, UC scenarios, etc. Those changes all had to go through proper procedures.

Note that all of these changes and questions would then generate the next round of feedback that required more changes.

Thus, any feedback short of obvious life-or-death mistakes was actively discouraged at that point.

After the rollout of version 1.0, with limited functionality, no one cared about documentation any more. There was simply so much of it.

Documentation ceased to be updated.

Developers were making a myriad of small changes every day, just to get the system up and running, while yesterday's batch of changes usually made something else break.

The final deadline was pushed back by a few months, and then again, several times, until further delays were no longer an option. The IT company in charge of the rollout had reluctantly agreed to support the system, no matter what.

Anti-Pattern

Documentation was elaborate right from the start. Thus, feedback on mockups caused many changes until the team wasn't able to update all the documents and models any more.

The system finally went live in full capacity, only to reveal more flaws. One by one, numerous parts of the system were completely reworked, based on direct feedback from angry end users.

That exact kind of reworking should have been avoided with mockups, so why it didn't work out?

There are many potential mistakes that I could point out, but they were management decisions and would require a separate book.

Within those constraints, there was not much that either analysts or UX designers could do (with mockups) to affect the outcome of the project.

Mockups are primarily a communication mechanism, ideally suited for early feedback. Where such approach is not possible, don't rely too much on mockups by themselves. Just *having* the mockups won't make much difference.

Anti-Patterns:
Mockups were not used early. Instead, they were only one of many outputs of a very formal analysis & design process.
Mockups were not created in quick iterations to obtain early feedback. Instead, they were presented monthly and feedback was discouraged.
Documentation was elaborate right from the start. Thus, feedback on mockups caused many changes until the team wasn't able to update all the documents and models any more.
Figure 15: Anti-patterns - ineffective use of mockups

CHAPTER 9

Choosing the Right Mockup Tool

Over the years, I have used many of the packages available, and what I have found is that two general capabilities make or break the effectiveness of any mockup tool:

- The speed with which you can crank out the results.

- Ease of use.

Raw speed is a prerequisite to working in short iterations, where mockups work best. Quick iterations allow you to test your ideas and quickly discard what doesn't work. Often, you do this together with your customer, so the process must be smooth.

Ease of use should be the same as making good old paper sketches. Active practitioners are usually highly efficient with main tools they use, but many people work with

What Makes an Effective Mockup Tool:

- The speed with which you can crank out the results.
- Ease of use.

mockups only occasionally and can't effectively utilize a tool that requires a course just to begin using it.

No effective mockup tool should be deficient in speed and ease of use. You want to focus on the work you are doing, rather than on the tool itself.

9.1 Checklists for Choosing a Mockup Tool

With the greater number of tools available in the market, we're starting to see increasing specialization. Take account of your specific needs when choosing the right tool for the job.

A word of warning here: avoid insisting on a feature just because it sounds cool, otherwise you could be limiting your choices too much. Meaning that you could end up buying the most expensive tools, which are necessarily the hardest to learn and use.

The choice is easier if you have a concrete project in mind. Think of that project (even imaginary one will do) and try to visualize your workflow and your needs. For example: will you be discussing rough throwaway mockups

What Do You Want the Tool For

- What is your workflow, i.e. how exactly do you intend to use the tool?
- What specific work outputs (e.g. printouts and exports) you require from the tool?

in live workshops, or will you be sending a detailed specification to customer for formal approval?

Checklist No.1: How will you be using the mockups
Do you need a tool for throwaway mockups or to produce something close to a spec?
Will non-programmers be using the tool? This may include analysts, interns, consultants, or customers. A tool for designers may be very different from a tool for developers.
Does the tool have good annotation facilities? These are crucial for both live workshops and for creating a specification.
Do you want to prototype right there in live workshops? The tool needs to be fast enough for that.
Will you aim for presenting real-life scenarios? If so, you need to be able to populate each element with realistic data easily.
Do you need to present your mockups in live workshops? You need to get your mockups in a slideshow then.
Will you be having lots of screens? If you are simulating scenarios, you could end up with hundreds. At that point, you need a tool to handle structure, templates, custom widgets, etc.
Figure 16: Mockup tool checklist — your process

Also, will you be developing pixel-perfect mockups for specific platform as high-res images, or will you be creating sketchy wireframes and exporting them and accompanying annotations to PDF?

Checklist No.2: How your mockups will look like. Also, what exports and formats do you need.
Does the tool have black and white look and feel? This is the single most important thing early in the project for initial mockups.
Do you need detailed mockups, rough sketches, or something in between?
What's your target platform? (desktop, web, smartphone, etc.)
Do you need the look and feel of a particular system for your mockups? The tool you choose should provide the appropriate skins.
Will you be creating simple screenshots or do you need exports, e.g. to PDF and Word?
Do you need to refine your spec even further? Often, the only viable option for this is to export to MS Word.
Do you need some basic interaction capability from your mockups? Most tools provide "links", so you can click on a button, etc., but some tools are almost fully interactive.
Figure 17: Mockup tool checklist — required work outputs

When you have answered the questions from both checklists, test various reputable tools that match your (now very specific) requirements. If in doubt, choose one that you feel comfortable with. After all, you will be the one spending time working with it.

There is another angle to consider here. Even if your later projects will be completely different, an adequate mockup tool will have already paid for itself many times over. At least from that standpoint, you can easily afford another one later, if it proves to be a better fit. Most analysts I know end up switching between several mockup tools, depending on the needs of their current project.

9.2 Overview of Available Tools

It doesn't seem like too long ago when I became frustrated with the tools that were available at the time. It was the main reason that I developed my own tool back in 2004.

Thankfully, the situation has changed and good choices are available now. At the time of writing, there is almost a hundred mockup tools out there. Some limited packages are even free.

On the other hand, most of the free and commercial options are still not very effective. One problem when looking for a tool is that most packages look the same until you have actually worked with them.

To give you a quick start, I'll mention several tools that in my opinion might be a good choice for different situations.

I won't go into details, because they change over time. I'll try to give you a general feel for a tool, instead.

First, there are the comprehensive tools. They are big and powerful, and will let you do virtually anything. The downside is a steep learning curve and a heavy price tag.

Comprehensive Tools: Powerful, but Expensive and Hard to Learn	
iRise www.iRise.com	A very comprehensive design platform for enterprises, if you can afford it.
Axure RP www.axure.com	Big and powerful, can do almost anything including interactive prototypes.
Justinmind Prototyper www.justinmind.com	Not as comprehensive as iRise or Axure, but quicker to learn.
Figure 18: Comprehensive mockup tools	

Next category are tools suitable for quick mockups and/or wireframes. Such tools are uniformly quick to learn, so much so that you can get results with many of them right away.

Quick Mockup and/or Wireframing Tools: Fast and Intuitive	
MockupScreens (my own tool) www.MockupScreens.com	Fast and easy to pick up. Exports quick specifications, and is primarily aimed at analysts.
Balsamiq Mockups www.balsamiq.com	User friendly and intuitive. Great for making any kind of wireframes.
MockFlow www.MockFlow.com	Fast and straight-forward. Optimized for web and mobile wireframes.
Pencil pencil.evolus.vn	Open source (free). Great when you need just a few quick sketches.
Figure 19: Quick mockup tools	

Many of the available tools are geared primarily toward graphic designers. You can use them successfully for other purposes, but you need to be aware of the differences.

Tools for designers are optimized for creating pixel-perfect mockups and some try to support design workflow in other ways, for example syncing of design assets.

I'm not a designer so I can't make any real recommendations. From my limited experience though:

Specialized Mockup Tools and Tools for Graphic Designers	
Proto.io www.proto.io	Online tool. Specializes for mobile and tablets, including creating realistic high-fidelity mockups. Some mobile specifics are e.g. gestures and transitions.
InvisionApp www.invisionapp.com	Realistic user experience prototypes. You import your own designs or mockups, make them interactive and collaborate to refine them further.
UXPin www.uxpin.com	A very powerful and collaborative UX (user experience) design tool that claims to cover the whole design process.
Figure 20: Specialized mockup tools	

> ## An Up-to-date List of Available Tools
>
> Below is the most comprehensive list of mockup and wireframing tools of which I am aware. Free and commercial tools are listed, as well as short informational sections and links:
>
> http://c2.com/cgi/wiki?GuiPrototypingTools

9.3 Frequently Asked Questions

Couldn't you use pen and paper for you mockups? If using a mockup tool, should it generate code directly from your mockups?

Below is my take on these and other frequently discussed topics, but solely from the perspective of quickly capturing software requirements.

9.3.1 Generating Code from Mockups?

People often ask why don't mockup tools produce actual code. Wouldn't it help jump-start development?

In practice the answer is no. During early stages of the project, you want to focus entirely on establishing a clear understanding with your customer. This is hard enough in itself, even without focusing at the same time on detailed inputs that a proper code generation would require.

> **Why Not Generate Code from Mockups?**
>
> You want to focus entirely on establishing a clear understanding with your customer.

9.3.2 Creating Fully Clickable Prototypes?

Some mockup tools produce fully clickable prototypes. Most don't, however.

This is because such prototypes require great amount of effort, which defeats the purpose of creating mockups. You want to rework your mockups repeatedly whenever you want to test a different approach.

> **Why Not Fully Clickable Prototypes?**
>
> They require too much effort to rework them rapidly and often.

Also, usually you don't really need an almost working prototype to discuss what fields and actions your client expects on a particular screen.

9.3.3 Why Not Use a Real GUI Builder?

With time, this particular discussion seems to have been settled on its own, so I'll just repeat the main points here.

Real GUI builders are:

- Much slower.

- Only programmers can use them - try explaining to an analyst how to populate a table in VB.

- They don't let you annotate your mockups on the fly.

- They don't provide black and white look to avoid being mistaken for an almost done application.

I realize that QT Designer and several others do have skins, but vast majority of them don't.

> **GUI Builders vs Specialized Mockup Tools**
>
> GUI builders are designed for programmers.
>
> Specialized tools are faster and communication oriented, including slideshows, annotations, etc.

Specialized mockup tools are usually:

- Communication-oriented, including slideshows, annotations, etc.

- Can print or export your mockups, and compile them with your notes into most standard formats, including PDF, HTML, DOC, etc.

- Better ones have some variant of "masters", so you can derive dozens of mockups from only a handful of basic application screens.

- Fast enough that you can prototype real-time in a meeting.

9.3.4 Using Plain Old Pen and Paper?

You can do that; it definitely works. However, when you get to the point of changing, tweaking, or maintaining these types of mockups, then you may really get stuck.

Thus, if you only need a few quick sketches, then pen and paper are perfectly fine, but be aware that this approach tends to get messy very fast.

What About Pen and Paper?

Those definitely work. However, changing and maintaing such mockups can get messy very fast.

Last Words

I hope that throughout the topics discussed in this book, you found something that you can start using right away.

Consider what you learned from this book and how that knowledge might be used in your particular context. Now, it's time to put this book down and apply your new knowledge on your own projects!

About the Author

Igor Ješe has been working in software development since the early 1990s, with an emphasis on software requirements and development methodology. Among other things, he is a certified Software Requirements Expert and a Project Management Professional.

He is also the author of MockupScreens, a commercial mockup tool. You can check it here:

http://www.MockupScreens.com

To read more of Igor's material on mockups, communication, software requirements, or software projects in general, check out his other website:

http://www.OnSoftwareProjects.com

List of Figures

Take-Aways by Chapter

Almost every page in this book provides quick take-aways. Their original purpose was to make it easier to scan the book and find a topic of immediate interest for the reader.

Since then, many readers have reported the take-aways useful by themselves, and asked for them in one place, easily printable if possible. Thus, I've compiled the take-aways in two ways:

1. On the following pages you'll find all the take-aways, chapter by chapter.

The problem is, a book format is not very useful for printing. Thus the second format:

2. You can download ready-for-print take-aways from this web-page:

http://www.mockups101.com/resources

Help Your Customers Understand What They Are Going to Get

Shooting At a Moving Target

1 Developers and customers don't understand each other.

Up-front specification is very time consuming and unfriendly to changes.

Short Mockup Iterations

2 They uncover issues immediately.

Requirements are agreed upon before the coding starts.

Basic Mockup Routine

Why Mockups

1 Everyone understands mockups.

Mockups are created fast and they are easy to rework.

Mockup Routine

2 1. Sketch several related screens.

2. Discuss them with customer.

3. Flesh out the details and repeat.

Make It Obvious That Mockups Are Not the Real Thing

Common Problems

1

False sense of progress.
Drowning in design feedback.
Team confused about the purpose of mockups.

Use Black and White Mockups Early On

2

People "know" what they see.
Sketchy mockups visually communicate it is a work-in-progress.

Provoking the Right Feedback

Techniques

1 Populate mockups with realistic data.

Put the issues in the spotlight.

Group screens to provide business context.

Use Black and White Mockups Early On

2 Data should be chosen to provoke a response.

Mocking-up whole scenarios tests your own understanding.

Discussing the Mockups Effectively

Present Mockups In Live Workshops

1 Tweak mockups together
with your customers.

You are producing the result together,
so it makes them care too!

Use Mockups to Test Ideas

2 Screen mockups test structure
and behavior.

Mock outputs test the visible results.

Mocking-Up the Outputs

Do Your Homework

1 Mock outputs need to be detailed.

Prepare a relevant sample of realistic data to work with.

Mock Outputs: Tips

2 Every part of the system should have outputs of some kind.

Use tools that your customers use, so they can clarify details among themselves.

Mockups as a Spec

Screen Sketches Are Not Enough

1

Empty your brain onto paper, then structure the information.
Develop your notes in parallel with your mockups.
Separate all the extraneous material into appendices.

Getting Results In Shortest Time Possible

2

Make a lot of on-screen notes.
Keep one step ahead of developers and be available.
Have your customer dedicate people for you.

Real World Case Studies

There Is No Single Best Way

1

Use what you understand, with clear and specific purpose.
When a process doesn't work for you, adjust it.

Take-Aways

2

Mockups need a quick turnaround to be effective.
Use real-life scenarios and data whenever you can.
Involve your customers from the very start.

Case Study: New Workflows

Challenge	Response
Workflows were completely new and therefore not well understood.	The mockup process won't stop at "proof-of-concept" stage, but will instead go for a full simulation of the system.
Deadlines were tight.	Customers' representatives actively participated in mockup development.
We needed to quickly test alternative ideas and establish what approach would work best.	Mockups were done in rapid micro-iterations.
We needed to be able to start from scratch when new realizations required it.	We focused on one workflow at a time, starting with "quick and dirty" mockups.
We needed to be able to test each workflow end-to-end, before the coding even started.	Detailed and realistic mock data sets were created, including paper inputs, reports, printouts, etc.
We didn't have the resources to develop a traditional specification.	Mockups were heavily annotated, to provide as much detail as feasible.
Developers had a lot of additional questions.	An analyst was attached to developers full-time, to elaborate on the mockups when needed.

Case Study: User Guide Before Coding

Challenge	Response
Project objectives entangled with out-of-scope issues.	Process (mockups) and scope limitations were backed by the customer's top-level executive.
Very limited budget.	The entire system was mocked-up and tested, including mock documents and cases.
How to communicate detailed solution to end users.	Mockups were turned into a User Guide. The Guide was organized into business scenarios displaying realistic data.
Main clients were accustomed to requesting customizations.	We involved main clients in the final iterations, asking them to volunteer.
Accepting late feedback was not possible.	We held a User Conference focused on getting immediate feedback.
Demonstrating good will without accepting late changes.	The most important feedback was accepted along with a number of cosmetic changes.
Clear understanding with the developers.	Developers were involved in mockup iterations, and they attended the User Conference.
User acceptance.	User acceptance was based on the User Guide and mock documents and cases used from the start.

A Cautionary Tale

1 Mockups are ideally suited for early feedback. Where such approach is not possible, just *having* the mockups won't make much difference.

Anti-Patterns

2 Mockups were not used early. Instead, they were only one of many outputs of a very formal analysis & design process.

Mockups were not created in quick iterations to obtain early feedback. Instead, they were presented monthly and feedback was discouraged.

Documentation was elaborate right from the start. Thus, feedback on mockups caused many changes until the team wasn't able to update all the documents and models any more.

Choosing the Right Mockup Tool

What Makes an Effective Mockup Tool

1
The speed with which you can crank out results.

Ease of use.

What Are Your Specific Requirements?

2
Most mockup tools target specific problems.

Know in advance what you want the tool for.

An Up-to-date List of Available Tools

3
http://c2.com/cgi/wiki?
GuiPrototypingTools

Mockup Tool Checklist 1: Process

How will you be using the mockups

Do you need a tool for throwaway mockups or to produce something close to a spec?

Will non-programmers be using the tool? This may include analysts, interns, consultants, or customers. A tool for designers may be very different from a tool for developers.

Does the tool have good annotation facilities? These are crucial for both live workshops and for creating a specification.

Do you want to prototype right there in live workshops? The tool needs to be fast enough for that.

Will you aim for presenting real-life scenarios? If so, you need to be able to populate each element with realistic data easily.

Do you need to present your mockups in live workshops? You need to get your mockups in a slideshow then.

Will you be having lots of screens? If you are simulating scenarios, you could end up with hundreds. At that point, you need a tool to handle structure, templates, custom widgets, etc.

Mockup Tool Checklist 2: Process

How your mockups will look like

Does the tool have black and white look and feel? This is the single most important thing early in the project for initial mockups.

Do you need detailed mockups, rough sketches, or something in between?

What's your target platform? (desktop, web, smartphone, etc.)

Do you need the look and feel of a particular system for your mockups? The tool you choose should provide the appropriate skins.

Will you be creating simple screenshots or do you need exports, e.g. to PDF and Word?

Do you need to refine your spec even further? Often, the only viable option for this is to export to MS Word.

Do you need some basic interaction capability from your mockups? Most tools provide "links", so you can click on a button, etc., but some tools are almost fully interactive.

Index